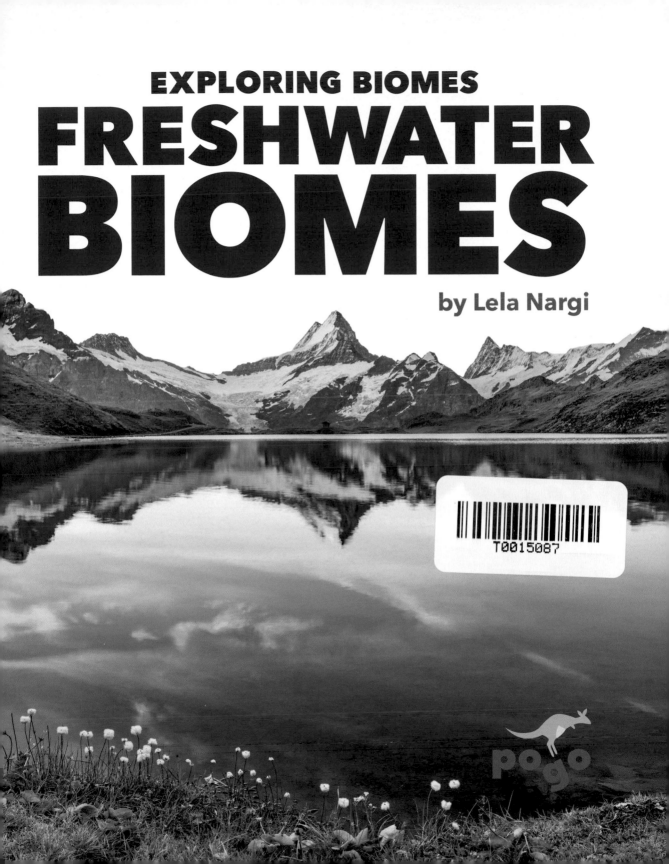

EXPLORING BIOMES
FRESHWATER BIOMES

by Lela Nargi

T0015087

Ideas for Parents and Teachers

Pogo Books let children practice reading informational text while introducing them to nonfiction features such as headings, labels, sidebars, maps, and diagrams, as well as a table of contents, glossary, and index.

Carefully leveled text with a strong photo match offers early fluent readers the support they need to succeed.

Before Reading

- "Walk" through the book and point out the various nonfiction features. Ask the student what purpose each feature serves.
- Look at the glossary together. Read and discuss the words.

Read the Book

- Have the child read the book independently.
- Invite him or her to list questions that arise from reading.

After Reading

- Discuss the child's questions. Talk about how he or she might find answers to those questions.
- Prompt the child to think more. Ask: Name two kinds of freshwater biomes. What are the similarities and differences between them?

Pogo Books are published by Jump!
5357 Penn Avenue South
Minneapolis, MN 55419
www.jumplibrary.com

Copyright © 2023 Jump!
International copyright reserved in all countries.
No part of this book may be reproduced in any form without written permission from the publisher.

Library of Congress Cataloging-in-Publication Data

Names: Nargi, Lela, author.
Title: Freshwater biomes / by Lela Nargi.
Description: Minneapolis, MN: Jump!, Inc., [2023]
Series: Exploring biomes | Includes index.
Audience: Ages 7-10
Identifiers: LCCN 2021055787 (print)
LCCN 2021055788 (ebook)
ISBN 9781636907567 (hardcover)
ISBN 9781636907574 (paperback)
ISBN 9781636907581 (ebook)
Subjects: LCSH: Freshwater ecology–Juvenile literature.
Freshwater biodiversity–Juvenile literature.
Classification: LCC QH541.5.F7 N37 2023 (print)
LCC QH541.5.F7 (ebook)
DDC 577.6–dc23/eng/20211117
LC record available at
https://lccn.loc.gov/2021055787
LC ebook record available at
https://lccn.loc.gov/2021055788

Editor: Eliza Leahy
Designer: Emma Bersie

Photo Credits: stocksolutions/Shutterstock, cover (left); Cocos.Bounty/Shutterstock, cover (right); Jojjik/Dreamstime, 1; spetenfia/Shutterstock, 3; goran_safarek/Shutterstock, 4; zhukovdima66/Shutterstock, 5; JUAN CARLOS MUNOZ/Alamy, 6-7; Katvic/Shutterstock, 8-9; Tom Tietz/Shutterstock, 10; Rostislav Stefanek/Shutterstock, 11; CHENG-WEI/Shutterstock, 12-13; All Canada Photos/Alamy, 14-15; Mike Cavaroc/Alamy, 16-17t; Jan Wlodarczyk/Alamy, 16-17b; Prapas Satong/Dreamstime, 18; Brocreative/Shutterstock, 19; Anton_dios/Shutterstock, 20-21; Eric Isselee/Shutterstock, 23.

Printed in the United States of America at Corporate Graphics in North Mankato, Minnesota.

TABLE OF CONTENTS

CHAPTER 1

FRESHWATER BODIES

Did you know Earth's **surface** is 75 percent water? Most of that is Earth's oceans. They are made of salt water. The rest is fresh water, like the water in lakes. It does not have much salt.

lake

glacier

Some fresh water is ice. **Glaciers** hold fresh water. Groundwater is fresh water found underground. It makes up most of the water we drink.

Everglades

There are many freshwater **biomes**. Fresh water makes up ponds, lakes, rivers, and streams. Ponds and lakes are still. Rivers and streams flow.

Wetlands can also hold fresh water. Florida's Everglades is one of the biggest freshwater wetlands in the world.

DID YOU KNOW?

Some lakes are big enough to have **tides**. The five Great Lakes have small tides. But strong winds can make big waves.

Freshwater bodies, such as lakes and ponds, started as dents in the land. Some dents were made by glaciers. Some were formed when Earth's **crust** moved. The dents filled with rain or snow. Or they filled with water from **springs**.

Lake Baikal in Russia was once a dent. Now it holds 20 percent of Earth's fresh water. It is 5,000 feet (1,525 meters) deep!

Lake
Baikal

CHAPTER 2

LIFE IN FRESH WATER

More than 100,000 kinds of plants and animals need fresh water for drinking or **habitat**. Animals like moose drink from lakes and ponds.

moose

Underwater, there is so much life. Tadpoles dart near the shore. Turtles swim to find food like small fish and snails. Bigger fish, like perch and pike, swim farther out. Carp eat water lily roots.

carp

Rivers start in hills or mountains. Trout and ducks swim at the headwaters. Rivers get wider as they flow down. River otters and mussels live in the middle. Ospreys hunt fish. The mouth flows into an ocean or other large body of water. Catfish and seals swim here.

osprey

TAKE A LOOK!

Rivers have three main parts. What are some animals that live in each part? Take a look!

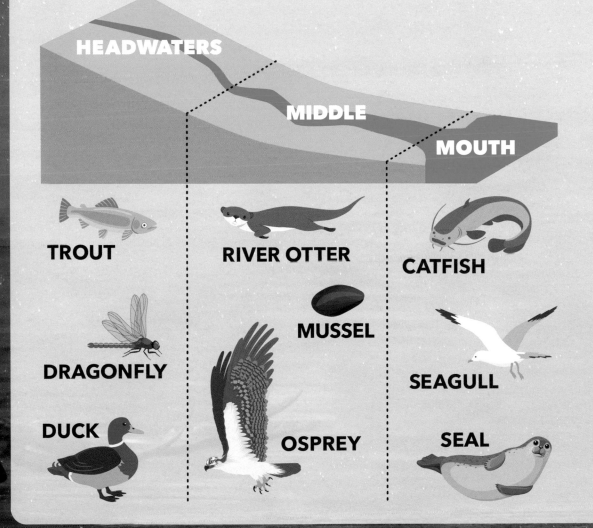

HEADWATERS

MIDDLE

MOUTH

TROUT

RIVER OTTER

CATFISH

DRAGONFLY

MUSSEL

SEAGULL

DUCK

OSPREY

SEAL

Many river mouths have wetlands. These are just right for baby birds. The water is warm and **shallow**. It is filled with crayfish and snakes to eat. Loons, swans, and seagulls build nests here.

loon

nest

Hudson River Estuary

mangrove forest

An **estuary** is where fresh water meets salt water. These are unique habitats. Much of New York's Hudson River is an estuary.

Mangrove forests grow in estuaries in the south. You can find them along Florida's coast.

DID YOU KNOW?

Estuaries are filled with **kelp** and grasses. They are safe places for salmon, crabs, and oysters to live and **reproduce**.

CHAPTER 3

FRESH WATER AND US

Humans need fresh water to drink. We get food, like fish, clams, and shrimp, from fresh water.

We also have fun in the water. In summer, we swim and water ski. In winter, we ice-skate on frozen lakes.

rain
barrel

Climate change is changing Earth's weather. Some places now get less snow or rain. This shrinks freshwater bodies.

One way to help is by collecting rainwater. You can save it to water plants. How else can you help save fresh water?

DID YOU KNOW?

There are many ways to save water. Take shorter showers. Reuse towels. Turn off the tap when you brush your teeth.

ACTIVITIES & TOOLS

TRY THIS!

MAKE YOUR OWN RIVER

Rivers and streams start in mountains and run down to the ocean. Make your own river and streams in this activity!

What You Need:
- sheet of white paper
- blue washable marker
- plastic container
- spray bottle filled with water

❶ Crumple the sheet of paper.

❷ Unfold it a little so it looks like a small mountain.

❸ Color the top ridges of your mountain with the marker.

❹ Put the mountain in a plastic container. Spray the mountain with water.

❺ Observe what happens to the water. Where does it go? How fast does it flow? The trickling water is the path the river takes down the mountain. Smaller trickles are streams. All the trickles are headed to the ocean.

GLOSSARY

biomes: Habitats and everything that lives in them.

climate change: Changes in Earth's weather and climate over time.

crust: The hard outer layer of Earth.

estuary: The wide part of a river, where it meets the ocean.

glaciers: Slow-moving masses of ice found in mountain valleys or polar regions.

habitat: A place where certain animals or plants are usually found.

kelp: A type of large brown seaweed.

mangrove: A kind of tree that grows in dense forests along estuaries, in salt marshes, and along coasts.

reproduce: To produce offspring.

shallow: Not deep.

springs: Places where water rises to the surface from underground sources.

surface: The outermost layer of something.

tides: The constant changes in sea level that are caused by the pull of the sun and moon on Earth.

wetlands: Areas of land where there is a lot of moisture in the soil.

INDEX

TO LEARN MORE

Finding more information is as easy as 1, 2, 3.

❶ **Go to www.factsurfer.com**

❷ **Enter "freshwaterbiomes" into the search box.**

❸ **Choose your book to see a list of websites.**

FACT SURFER